FIGURES IN CHINA'S SPACE INDUSTRY

Who is Lin Shi'e?

www.royalcollins.com

FIGURES IN CHINA'S SPACE INDUSTRY

Who is Lin Shi'e?

By Ye Qiang and Dong Pingping

Books Beyond Boundaries
ROYAL COLLINS

In 1931, the September 18 Incident
(Manchurian Incident) occurred, marking
the Japanese invasion of Manchuria in
northeast China. Lin Shi'e, who was studying at
Shanghai Jiao Tong University, saw the sufferings his
country endured under foreign abuse. As the war went on,
Lin's school was forced to close; his classmates were ready to fight the
enemy with bare hands. Lin stood up and said: "Our country's weakness is
the real reason for the foreign attack. We should devote ourselves to military
construction, enhancing national strength with knowledge and technology.
Let us apply what we have learned to save our country!" His classmates all
supported his proposal.

3

With the idea to save his country through aerospace engineering, Lin traveled to the United States to study at the Massachusetts Institute of Technology (MIT) with Charles Stark Draper, a world-famous scientist and gyroscopic instrument expert. During his doctoral studies, he published a paper in the *Journal of Mathematics and Physics of MIT*, in which he creatively proposed the "Lin method for finding roots of algebraic equations by using long divisions iteratively." It is the only mathematical method named after a Chinese person. In 1939, Dr. Lin Shi'e graduated from MIT and returned to China. He wanted to dedicate all he had learned to his home country.

After the war, the People's Republic of China was founded. But Lin Shi'e knew he had not yet completed his mission to save the country through aerospace engineering. It was clear that China could only become strong and prosperous with her own aviation learning institute, and professionals who could pass down the heritage of the Chinese aerospace industry.

In October 1952, the Central Committee issued a document to establish the Beijing Institute of Aeronautics (now Beihang University). As one of the school's founders, this brought immense happiness and aspiration to Lin Shi'e.

Since then, Lin Shi'e has worked at the Beijing Institute of Aeronautics for many years. With his profound knowledge and active academic thinking, he has taught more than one thousand undergraduate students and personally advised more than twenty graduate students. After graduation, these students have entered the fields of aviation, aerospace, navigation, and others, gradually becoming the pillars of New China.

In November 1958, Lin Shi'e established China's first gyro inertial navigation research laboratory. The laboratory mainly focused on the liquid floating gyro as a research object in its primary stage. It was a time of minimal materials, poor scientific research conditions, and a lack of communication. Lin Shi'e and his colleagues had to overcome unimaginable difficulties to complete this prototype.

In order to make the rotor float, Lin Shi'e experimented at home over and over again, even thinking about the problem while walking. One day, when he was resting in his room, his wife knocked on the door to call him to lunch.

15

Lin Shi'e came to the kitchen and saw some starch and water on the table. Suddenly, he had an idea. He made a starch-water mixture for the experimental floating liquid but found it unsuccessful. Then, he picked up the salt and mixed it with water, but it failed him again. Unwilling to give up the search for the perfect ingredient, he turned and saw the sugar. As he shook the cup of sugar water, he was surprised to observe the rotor float.

Excitedly, he ran out of the kitchen shouting, "Sugar water! It's sugar water!" The sugar water experiment inspired Lin Shi'e's research on the liquid floating gyroscope. After that, he was affectionately referred to as "professor sugar water." Finally, Lin Shi'e and his team successfully built a prototype for a liquid floating gyro.

During his decades of teaching and his research career, Lin Shi'e has always put the country's needs at heart, and he taught his students to cherish this hard-earned stability and unity through personal experience. Lin often said to them: "You are young. You should make a greater contribution to the people."

In 1986, Lin Shi'e said goodbye to his beloved classrooms and lecture halls because of his poor physical health. However, he still encouraged students to work hard and contribute to national construction during his time in the hospital. Lin was very concerned about China's reunification, and he did a lot of meaningful work for the early reunion of families and friends across the Taiwan Strait.

23

Lin Shi'e passed away on September 27, 1987. This venerable teacher, scientist, and patriot has left us a precious spiritual legacy from his 74 years of beautiful life.

Acquire and adopt; it is the way to use and transform. Lin Shi'e has exercised the wisdom of this idiom throughout his life – in his extraordinary achievements as a student, in his innovative contribution to aviation instruments and gyro inertial navigation as a researcher, and in his devotion to educating the next generation of aerospace professionals as a teacher. Lin is still influencing young people today with the words, "Love China, love aerospace."

25

About the Authors

Ye Qiang studied oil paintings at Sichuan Fine Arts Institute. After graduating in 2001, he began teaching as an associate professor in the department of New Media Art and Design at Beihang University. Ye's paintings have been displayed in hundreds of national and international exhibitions, and he has held solo exhibitions in galleries, including the Shanghai Art Museum, several times. Ye's paintings and scholarship can be found in more than 20 academic journals and monographs. He has also published seven textbooks.

Dong Pingping is Vice-Secretary of the Party Committee and a member of the Supervisory Commission of the department of New Media Art and Design at Beijing University of Aeronautics and Astronautics.

Figures in China's Space Industry:
Who is Lin Shi'e?

Written by Ye Qiang and Dong Pingping

First published in 2023 by Royal Collins Publishing Group Inc.
Groupe Publication Royal Collins Inc.
BKM Royalcollins Publishers Private Limited

Headquarters: 550-555 boul. René-Lévesque O Montréal (Québec) H2Z1B1 Canada
India office: 805 Hemkunt House, 8th Floor, Rajendra Place, New Delhi 110 008

Original Edition © Shaanxi People's Education Press Co., Ltd.

ISBN: 978-1-4878-1107-5

To find out more about our publications, please visit www.royalcollins.com.